1 MONTH OF
FREE
READING

at

www.ForgottenBooks.com

By purchasing this book you are eligible for one month membership to ForgottenBooks.com, giving you unlimited access to our entire collection of over 700,000 titles via our web site and mobile apps.

To claim your free month visit:
www.forgottenbooks.com/free78897

ISBN 978-0-484-45074-4
PIBN 10078897

THE MONEY CRISIS:

ITS

CAUSES AND REMEDY.

BY

ALFRED YAPLE.

CINCINNATI:
ROBERT CLARKE & CO.
1873.

THE MONEY CRISIS:

CAUSES AND REMEDY.

To ascertain the causes of the present financial condition of the country is essential to the discovery and adoption of the proper remedy.

That something can not be made by men from nothing; that to assume that any number of so-called cents less than one hundred is a dollar is false; that a government can create or possess no wealth other than that given to it by the people from their stores; that the wealth of a people consists only of the surplus of their productions, or creations of labor remaining after all that they consume or destroy is deducted; that the finite is not infinite, or the limited unlimited, and that the wealth and resources of any people or nation can be exhausted, are axiomatic truths. When, then, any government finds itself without the means to pay the expenses of all the undertakings in which it is engaged, and, in lieu thereof, emits its promises to pay in any form, it anticipates the existing wealth in the hands of the people, or what they are to produce and save in the future, or both: and they are finite. And such promises must be intrinsically as much less in value than real money, the measure of all values, as the interest for the shortest time possible to collect the money from the people and pay such promises will amount to. When any government adopts the policy of issuing such

anticipatory promises, it may do so to the extent of all
the wealth of the country, and all that the existing and
future generations of the people may thereafter produce.
If such promises bear no interest, and they be so nu-
merous that none of them can be paid sooner than six-
teen and two-third years (supposing the rate of interest
to be six per cent.), they are practically worthless—the
present worth of a dollar bearing no interest for that
time being reckoned zero.   This will guide us in fixing
such values for intermediate periods.   If such anticipations be funded, *i. e.*, put in the shape of interest-
bearing bonds, then, if the government shall continue
stable and strong enough to coerce the payment of taxes
to pay such interest in money as it falls due, such debt
will have a present value, however long it may have to
run, even though the property and earnings of the present and the coming generation may not be sufficient to
pay the principal.   The danger, in such case, to be ap-
prehended, would be the stability and strength of the
government; for the coming generation might think that
its predecessor had been too greedy in its endeavor, not
only to consume all its own property and earnings, but
also that of the succeeding: they might think that it
was against nature for one generation of men to appro-
priate to themselves the earnings of all men in future
times, leaving them simply to toil for the dead ; that
the old hive had no right to devour all the honey to be
made by its future swarms.   The realization of this
condition of things renders the idea of a tyrannical government with its iron hand of force—a standing army—
congenial to a sense of safety and the security of in-
comes.

If such government promises (anticipations of future

resources) be made a legal tender—that is, if people
be compelled to receive the promised dollar as and for
an actual dollar, when it must, in its very nature, be
worth less—the debtor class are at first the gainers of
the difference in value between the two, and the plan
begins with immense popularity; and as it is so much
easier to promise than to create, the scheme is sure to
be overdone. The example is catching. Such issues
being superabundant, lead the people into feverish
schemes of wild speculation and enterprises, to carry
out which they issue their promises based upon the an-
ticipated gains of such undertakings. They call these
promises "stocks," etc.; and all are soon deceived by
the supposition that such debts are wealth, and act ac-
cordingly, until the mistake is discovered by the failure
to receive any interest on them. Then they find all
mere debt—worthless promises by somebody to pay—
anticipations impossible of realization. If th government attempts to retrace its steps, and work its promises up to the value of their face in money, it can only
do so by exacting from the people, in the shape of
taxes, part of their actual wealth already created and in
hand, which must produce greater or less distress; and
then, also, the debtor class has to pay to the creditor
class as much more per dollar as the value of the promise increases; the process is now changed, the engine
reversed. Thus, say one hundred and twelve dollars
in legal tenders is to-day only worth one hundred dollars in gold. The debtor buys on the legal-tender
basis; his debt falls due a year hence, when, we will
suppose, the action of the government has made the
paper equal to gold: the debtor must pay one hundred
and twelve dollars in gold, or its value, when, if values

had remained as at the time of his contract, he would
have only to pay one hundred and twelve dollars in
paper of the value of one hundred dollars in gold. He
loses twelve dollars in gold by the system adopted.
Resumption of specie payments makes the debtor class
pay the difference between paper and gold during the
entire continuance of the process. It would be instruc-
tive, were it germain to the present purpose of the
writer, to show how this, together with other necessary
parts of the system—interest-bearing bonds, banks created with and upon the debt, and high tariffs—tends,
inevitably, to prevent the man who earns the dollar
from keeping it, and to vest the wealth of a country in
few hands. Another effect is to divert the energies of
men from real business to be employed in mere
wagering.

The almost daily contraction and expansion of the
value of such promises, as compared with coin, tempts
to " betting " on the value upon a given future day,
which buying and selling " short " simply is. Combi-
nations—" rings "—are then formed to affect values at
given times, from which real interests suffer. More
grain and pork, gold and produce of all kinds, are, in
form, bought and sold than there is in the land, the
parties never expecting to deliver or receive any of the
article, but only to pay or take the difference between
the contract and the then market price. With a fixed
measure of values, fluctuations would be too little to
admit of heavy gambling. But, with the credit standard,
all real business, that founded upon the actual gold and
property of the country, is at the mercy of such
gamesters, when the actual property of the land, affected

only by the laws of supply and demand, ought to
regulate markets.

The evil is greatly increased, if the surplus promises
be funded in various classes of bonds. Then "rings,"
who are able to choose or control government agents,
favor one class to-day and reap gain, another to-morrow
and reap more. This was well illustrated (except that
no charge of combination between government officers
and "rings" is intended to be made) during the
present crisis. . The government gave currency for all
bonds of former issues, except ten-forties. This -at
once lessened their value. Besides greatly promoting
wagering, the system of issuing more than one class of
interest-bearing debt is a mistake. It is condemned by
every political economist, and defended by none. It is
an admission that the financier does not know the value
of his own government's credit, but is experimenting.
His first loan, that most favorable to the creditor, he
may work off. This then competes with the next in
series in the world's market, and thus the nation's
credit is made to fight itself. Ex-Treasurer Boutwell's
last scheme is peculiarly liable to this objection. But,
as no business can be successfully carried on indefinitely
upon what one owes instead of what he owns, upon
what he hopes to realize instead of what he has—as, for
instance, a corn or cotton raiser can not prosper by
anticipating *now* his next two, three, or half-dozen
crops—so the country, whose people have ultimately to
pay it, can not permanently flourish upon the business
basis of the government's debt. By concentration and
by binding all business up in the plan, it will last
longer; but, in the end, the fall is so much the higher
and harder, and the wreck and ruin so much the more

complete. This has been the universal experience of mankind, and is demonstratively inevitable. But, while the system lasts, before it has begun to decline, men never have been convinced of the fact, it being so much more easy and agreeable to anticipate than to realize.

They therefore cherish the delusion that, in the given instance, their affairs are exempt from the operation of inevitable and unchanging laws. But, after the system of anticipating or borrowing from the future has been carried beyond reasonable limits, then every new resort to it by issuing further promises produces immediate and very observable evils. Such additional promises merely lessen the purchasing power of the aggregate mass of promises already out to an amount equal to the increased issue, and nothing is really gained in the present, while the burden for the future is increased just so much. This is not the case so long as the limit to which debt may be safely incurred, has not been reached.

One terrible consequence follows—the best part of the productive classes are immediately injured. All who are engaged in raising, manufacturing, and handling natural products from the time seed is sown, a tree cut down, or a stone quarried until the article reaches the hands of the ultimate consumer or user, are producers or creators of property and wealth. The best part of these have permanent employment, and therefore a fixed rate of wages—a salary. Every new issue of promises, circulating as money, lessens so much the purchasing power of such wages, and thus takes off so much from it. And while such issues thus positively tax productive labor, they do not give any real relief to others; for lessening their value still more than formerly, and thus driving coin farther away from circulation (it being a truth that if there be two kinds of dollar, or guineas or pounds, the cheapest only will circulate as money), the paradoxical condition of things will exist that there is both too much and too little money in circulation, and increase simply gives a correspondingly less purchasing power.

This system can sustain itself longer in the United States than in a country whose resources are fully developed, and especially than in one having no productive mines of the precious metals. It is a demonstrable fact—a fact conceded by political economists—that the adoption of a paper-promise system of money, including all amounts, from the largest to the smallest, will drain, if continued, the nation adopting it of all its precious metals. The products of our gold and silver mines have gone abroad to enable us to float our paper at home, together with a large amount of gold and silver we had on hand when the paper-promise system was adopted. I think there is some $50,000,000 less now than then; but this does not give an adequate idea of the inevitable drain. At first our debt was owned by our own people; but it was funded in bonds, payable in coin, the great mass of which was taken abroad, for which gold in hand was realized. These, with constant interest, have yet to be paid in gold, which will go abroad, and thus we can form some idea of the inevitable drain of the system. To the extent of their productions our gold and silver mines have ameliorated the situation. Next, the resources of our country are not half developed, and "flush times" always quicken human energies, and, in such a country, lead to the development of natural resources, and this insures larger production. From this, however, must be deducted increased waste; people under such circumstances always become more extravagant. This extravagance reaches the producing classes as well as others, while many turn mere gamblers, cloaking their real calling under the respectable appellation of business. But sooner or later the system must fail; a settlement forces itself; a crash is the result, and suffering, misery, and ruin are wide-spread and everywhere. Our present system was not, by Mr. Chase, its founder, and our wisest financiers, expected to last longer than the close of the war, when a general crash was anticipated; but gold production, an undeveloped country, and the sale of our bonds abroad by Secretary McCulloch, at a cheap present rate (for gold), at a high rate of interest, averted the catastrophe for a few years, to make it all the worse when it should come. To give another dram to the inebriate can not prevent threatened *delirium tremens.* It has been found as impossible to create something out of nothing as to achieve "perpetual motion," or to "square the circle."

After the system was adopted and before a safe limit of debt had been reached or passed, but enough incurred to enable debtors to pay less than they owed and be released, while property seemed to rise as the money with which it was bought fell in value, and every man's credit was taken instead of requiring from him money, it was vain to attempt to argue the system—many shrewd ones were making money by it and all thought they were. That settled the fate of argument. It was voted mere "speculative theory," having no application to our particular case. After such limits had been passed, the subject became too dangerous to discuss.

It could no more be touched than the slavery question in the South just before and during, the late war. It might bring ruin, and though ruin to thousands was inevitable some day, each man, who, if it came then, would be involved in it, expected to get safe before it would come of its own accord. Then for a statesman to say, "The way to resume specie payments is to resume," was instant political annihilation.

Another thing has tended greatly to popularize the system adopted by us. The non-interest bearing portion of the debt was put in the shape of currency, and all local emissions were taxed out of existence. This gave uniformity to the value of such currency throughout the entire country. This has been seen and felt by everybody from the first, and the weakness of the foundation upon which the superstructure rests has been unheeded. Had such currency been redeemable in coin, at the will of the holder, without loss, then, indeed, would it have been the best shape in which a large part of the public debt could exist; for it would be drawing no interest, and, at the same time, furnish a safe and uniform currency, less bulky and costly to transport than gold.

The aggregation of such elements, and the shift by which we realized a large present amount of gold from Europe by the sale of bonds on which we pay a high rate of interest, and must yet pay the principal, the full face of the bond, causes a general belief that it has been, upon the whole, one of the wisest and best systems of finance ever devised by man, and without which we could not have successfully prosecuted the late war and preserved the Union. This theory has the advantage of having been tried, while no other, though it might have been far better, more economical and efficient, was.

Its real merits and defects will never be realized until the system shall have worked out all its necessary results. It is a fact, that by its adoption, the war was carried on for two years and a half without the levy and collection of a cent of tax, except a small real-estate one, which it was soon found could not be made legally valid or enforcible beyond the limits of the federal authority, there being no allegiance due to the government from those it was unable to protect in the revolted states. This caused such promises to depreciate, and the government to promise to pay a dollar for every half-dollar's worth, or less, that it obtained; and, hence, virtually doubled its expenses. Taxation was not resorted to, because our then rulers were timid, afraid the people would not submit to taxation; when the truth turned out to be that the courage and self-sacrificing spirit of the people were far greater than the authorities possessed. But for the people the struggle would have been given up. But there was not one hour from the time Sumter was fired upon until the surrender of Lee and Johnston, that peace could have been made upon the basis of separation, and those making it allowed to live in the country for a single day. The feeling and disposition of the people was, then, wholly misunderstood at the start. When, therefore, Mr. Chase, as secretary of the treasury, in December, 1862, recommended the adoption of the system, James Gallatin, a banker of New York, and son of Albert Gallatin, urged upon his attention the feasibility of maintaining specie payments by a proper system of taxation, which would accomplish our purposes fully, and make the war cost far less. The then subtreasury law authorized the issuing of government notes, payable on demand, which, with an immediate and effective system of taxation, Gallatin thought would carry the government safely through. What evidence have we that it would not? What that it would? Great examples are before us. The methods adopted in Europe, by the different states, for carrying on the great wars growing out of the French Revolution. Take, for example, France and England, and commence with the first consulship of Napoleon, in 1799. Napoleon was a prodigy in his ability to comprehend, instantaneously, the existence and strength of resources, and to combine and use them. This made him too bold and direct for a successful diplomat, and his boundless ambition to rule the world prevented him from conceding anything. These were his defects.

When he reached the Tuileries, on the first night of his consulship, his attendant remarked: " Well, we are here." " Yes," said Napoleon, "but this is nothing; how to stay here is what is to be considered." He met there all the ministers of public affairs and others, celebrated political economists. He found that the previous directory had declared bankruptcy on the revolutionary debt, with all its forced paper assignats. There were also outstanding debts for the years five, six, and seven. The assessments for the year six had not even been made out, and not more than one-third for the year seven. All for the year eight was to be met. He could not obtain a loan for more than 12,000,000 francs—hardly sufficient for a single day. War was being carried on in Egypt: Moreau, with a large army, was on the Rhine; war in Italy; La Vendee unsettled;

civil war in France; all the armies long unpaid. He
was anxiously inquired of, by his baffled and appalled
statesmen, as to what he intended to do. He replied:
"I shall pay cash, or pay nothing." Upon this plan
he set to work, dividing tax assessments into many
short installments, so that those who paid scarcely per-
ceived that they were burdened. For the year nine,
after meeting all except the revolutionary debt, he had
the cash basis. In the year nine he shouldered and
funded the revolutionary debt, and met everything in
cash. Not only this, but he began the repair of the
roads, neglected for ten years. During this time he conducted, in person, the campaign ending at Marengo.
In 1803 he made his vast preparations for the invasion
of England. This system forced the most rigid economy in every department. Reckless men and mere
speculators were driven from the field, and honest and
prudent men occupied their places.

But he was often sorely pressed with the need of
money. He declined so expensive a process as a resort to borrowing. There was another way to borrow—
to run in debt to the contractors, not paying them in
full. They were anxious for the adoption of this
course, but he thought it more expensive than regular
borrowing. They would be sure to get twice or thrice
paid, furnish inferior articles and at their own chosen
times and in their own way, giving as an excuse that
they could not do otherwise, because unpaid. He de-
termined to pay the contractors regularly, and to require
them to furnish supplies regularly and at reasonable
rates. But war came from all quarters, so that England
escaped invasion. In 1805 the victories of Ulm and
Austerlitz, and the naval defeat of Trafalgar followed:

Jena and Eylau in 1806; Friedland and the peace of Tilsit in 1807. But once during this time was there a suspension, lasting but a few days, caused by the united merchants taking advantage of the minister, Marbois, whom Napoleon indorsed as honest, but dismissed for having made a mistake. At this time, 1805, and after the coalition of all the European powers against Napoleon, it was proposed to resort to paper promises, but Napoleon wrote to Marbois, "While I live I will not issue any paper." He kept his word. France soon acquired the gold, and consequently commanded the markets of the world. Failing to get the command of the sea by the result of the naval battle of Trafalgar, and outnumbered more than five to one, Napoleon was finally defeated by combined Europe, but France suffered no financial crisis. When Napoleon was sent to Elbe, and after Waterloo, banished to St. Helena, there was not even a ripple in financial circles. France has ever since adhered to a specie basis,* the system of Napoleon, which, like one of his military plans, remaining invincible as long as it can be clearly identified. France of to-day has paid her debt to Germany in gold, and has sold her bonds to her own people, who hold them, for gold. They bear, too, a low rate of interest. Ours is in magnitude a European debt, bearing an American rate of interest. Until the time comes to pay the principal of a debt, the rate of interest it bears fixes its weight upon the country. $1,000,000 at six per cent. is just as burdensome to a people as $2,000,000 at three per cent.

---

* The Bank of France has *nominally* suspended on account of the German war, but its paper has not depreciated, but it has had the effect of transferring French balances to the Bank of England.

England, on the contrary, adopted the legal-tender system, and piled up such a debt as has prevented her ever since from venturing upon any great enterprise, while at the close of the war she was visited with a terrible financial crash and general bankruptcy. Read the works of Burke and Napier's Peninsular War, to learn the evils of the English system. The latter, speaking of the Peninsular war, which began in 1808, contrasts the condition of England and France. "Then England," he says, "had those twin curses; paper money and public credit—strength in the beginning, but weakness in the end—which were recklessly used by statesmen whose policy regarded not the interests of posterity, whose system snatched the means of the many to bribe a few in order to misgovern all." The Bank of England, it may here be observed, suspended specie payments from 1797 to 1819, being forbidden by government to so redeem its paper issues. The bank was so prudently managed, however, that its paper did not materially depreciate for ten years. In 1825 came the inevitable crash.

Of France, Napier says: "Her manufactures were rapidly improving, her internal and continental traffic was robust, her debt small, her financial operations conducted on a prudent plan and with exact economy" (which is the necessary consequence of a specie basis in a time when much money is required, while the very opposite is the case when credit is used instead of money); "her supplies were all raised within the year without any great pressure from taxation, and from a sound metallic currency." We copied, and for twelve years have practiced upon England's admitted and lamentable mistake—its blunder, which was a crime.

THE REMEDY.

When a government has once adopted a system of finance, every body who desires to do any business at all, must do it under the adopted system. Therefore, when evils fall upon the people from the fatalities resulting from a defective system, it becomes the duty of all, while seeking for a safer basis, so to proceed as to protect all as far as possible and to cause no unnecessary distress. Enough of that will ensue at best. In seeking a remedy, we at once direct our attention to a specie basis; and here it will become necessary to remove a generally accepted opinion, the result of fallacious assertions made to prop up and continue the paper-credit system, that there is not sufficient gold to maintain such specie basis. This assertion has been accepted without proof. The fact is, that, since the discoveries of gold in California and Australia, that metal has, in reality, become too abundant for the requirements of currency. It has lost much of its purchasing power. In 1803, in France, the quantities of gold and silver in the world were approximately ascertained, and the value of gold fixed at ~~fourteen~~ and one-half times its weight in silver; when as early as 1859, upon a similar investigation, it was found to be worth not more than eleven and one-half times its weight in silver. (See Cobden's translation of Chevalier on Gold.) The reason none is in circulation in the United States, is because we have a cheaper money, which ever takes the field, banishing the more valuable. A gold basis at once brings all the gold coin in circulation.

Let Congress, then, ignoring all special interests and

classes, and looking alone to the well-being of the whole country, devise a wise and just system of internal taxation, and a tariff whose object shall be the realization of the greatest amount of revenue instead of merely fostering, by so-called protection, certain interests.   Then, let the legal-tender notes be made redeemable in coin, at their face, at the will of the holder. As they will furnish a uniform currency, and be less bulky and weighty than gold, and consequently cheaper to transport, they will be at a slight premium as between them and gold.   This will shove all the gold into the channels of circulation, it being the cheaper, and will prevent the presentation of "greenbacks" for redemption at all; while the latter will be a debt of the government, bearing no interest.

But it will be said that the national-bank issues are in the way, that they can not redeem their bills in gold. It is true they can not.   A bank, whose paper promise the day it is issued, is worth less than its face in gold, never can afford to allow it to become worth gold; for it would have to pay (lose) the difference.   It may become less valuable—never more. As well might a bridge built with a "swag" in the bottom chord be expected to get "camber," or "bow up" by use— organic structure renders that impossible.

But these bank charters are amendable or repealable at any time.   Now, say the owners of a national bank have bought and paid for one hundred thousand dollars in registered bonds, deposited them in the federal treasury, and received from it ninety thousand dollars in bills to circulate; these it has used, and, while doing so, has drawn interest from the treasury upon the entire one hundred thousand dollars of its bonds: it breaks;

the government then assumes its circulation, having in hand the one hundred thousand dollars in bonds to indemnify it for so doing. Now, suppose the government should assume *all* the bank issues as part of its own "greenback" issue, and cancel a corresponding amount of the deposited bonds, the value to be fixed fairly on the basis of some past date: it would simply be turning a part of its interest-bearing debt into a non-interest-bearing debt—a thing that it virtually does when one of these banks fails. Then take away the right from these banks to issue bank-bills as currency, and provide a heavy prohibitory tax upon all local-bank issues, and it does seem to the writer that we would very soon reach a sound and prosperous basis, and have the best paper currency, so long as the public debt shall last, in the world.

But it will be said, " How can the debtor class pay one hundred and twelve dollars in gold for what they agreed only to pay one hundred dollars in gold, or one hundred and twelve dollars in legal tenders." The answer is obvious, we have had one name, "dollar," for two different values. Give the creditor the very *value* he contracted for, and oblige the debtor to pay that, and no less, nor any more. Do not stick at names or words, but consider values. We know the value of the "greenback," as compared with gold, upon every day since such notes were issued. Make the debtor pay the gold value of his promise at the time it ~~became due~~ *was*, with lawful interest. The school-boy who has worked sums " in exchange " in his arithmetic, is able to comprehend the plan at once. He can tell, their relative values being given, how many *dollars* are to be paid for one thousand *thalers*. If this be not done, the strain of the

crisis will constantly be upon the weakest part, the
debtor class, whom it must grind to powder, and with
theirs, bring general ruin.   The government, however,
has promised to pay " dollars," and it must redeem its
promises in good faith.   Not to do so, would bring
upon us far greater evils than could be compensated for
by any immediate gains.   No " scaling," therefore, by
it of its own debts, no shaving of its own paper as has
been heretofore constantly done.

These observations are submitted, not in the belief
that they embody perfection, but in the hope that they
will, to some extent, serve to call the attention of wise
and experienced men of all parties to this subject, and
induce them to devise adequate remedies for the financial
diseases of the times—a matter in which everybody in the
land is vitally interested.

Colquhoun—Roman Civil Law. p. 153,
In all loans, the principle of repayment is,
that that which has been lent shall
rendered at the same mere intrinsic
ch it bore at the time of its receipt
If the value have been raised,
tor has not so many pieces to pay,
crease or diminution of value, legally
equivalent, as regards the subjec
State, to such change in value"

' ten in

CPSIA information can be obtained
at www.ICGtesting.com
Printed in the USA
BVHW04*0034180818
524721BV00025B/2529/P